DISCARD

DISCARD

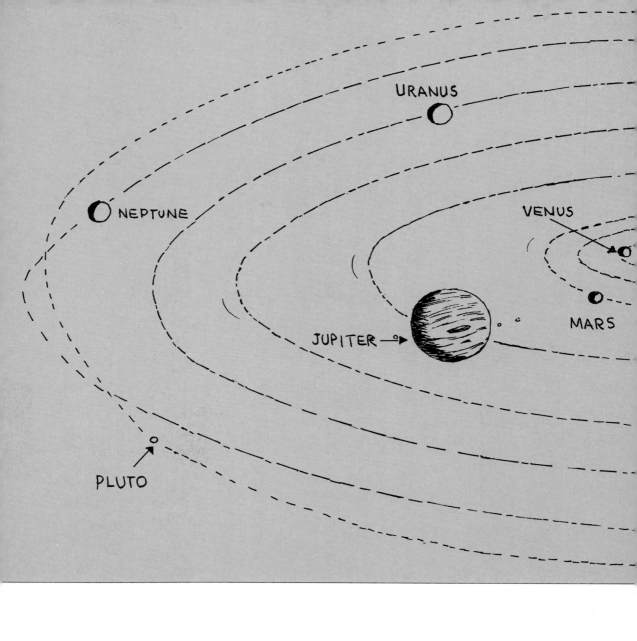

BY *Franklyn M. Branley*

ILLUSTRATED BY LEONARD KESSLER

THOMAS Y. CROWELL   NEW YORK

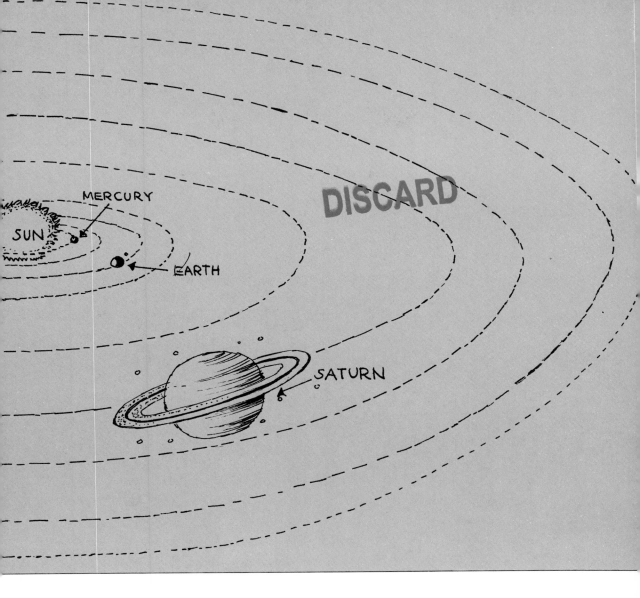

SUN

MERCURY

EARTH

SATURN

DISCARD

SATURN

The Spectacular Planet

J
523.46
B

45611

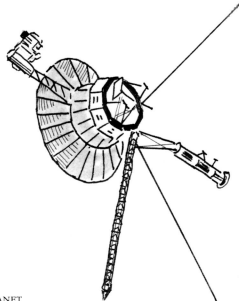

SATURN: THE SPECTACULAR PLANET

Text copyright © 1983 by Franklyn M. Branley
Illustrations copyright © 1983 by Leonard Kessler

All rights reserved. No part of this book may be
used or reproduced in any manner whatsoever without
written permission except in the case of brief quotations
embodied in critical articles and reviews. Printed in
the United States of America. For information address
Thomas Y. Crowell Junior Books, 10 East 53rd Street,
New York, N.Y. 10022. Published simultaneously in
Canada by Fitzhenry & Whiteside Limited, Toronto.

Library of Congress Cataloging in Publication Data
Branley, Franklyn Mansfield, 1915–
    Saturn.

    Summary: Describes the physical features and charac-
teristics of the "Queen of the Planets" and its satellites,
and presents theories about the rings of Saturn.
    1. Saturn (Planet)—Juvenile literature.   [1. Saturn
(Planet)]   I. Kessler, Leonard P., date   ill.
II. Title.
QB671.B7   523.4'6   81-43890
ISBN 0-690-04213-2   AACR2
ISBN 0-690-04214-0 (lib. bdg.)

10 9 8 7 6 5 4 3 2 1
First Edition

Contents

Introduction   1

Before the Space Probes   2

Pioneer and *Voyager*   8

The Size and Shape of Saturn   10

Rotation and Revolution   12

Heat and Temperature   14

Density, Mass, and Gravity   17

The Layers of Saturn   21

The Rings of Saturn   27

Theories about the Rings   30

Saturn's Satellites   34

Finding Saturn in the Night Sky   48

Index   52

*(Color photograph insert begins
after page 26.)*

Since the early 1960s we have been sending probes far out into space. Unmanned spacecraft have traveled millions and millions of miles to distant planets, flying past them and in some cases even landing on them. The probes have shown us striking views of the cratered surface of Mercury, the dense clouds that surround Venus, the deep valleys and riverbeds on Mars, and the fierce storms that rage on Jupiter. And they have given us close-range views of the rings of Saturn.

Each of the nine planets in our solar system is different in one way or another from the rest—in surface appearance, for example, in temperature, or in the gases it contains. Yet the most unusual and impressive of all the planets is Saturn, because of its rings. There may be as many as a thousand of them. Some people believe there are even more than that. It is this elaborate system of rings that makes Saturn the spectacular planet it is.

BEFORE THE SPACE PROBES

Long before there were planetary probes, or even telescopes, people knew about Saturn. Looking into a clear, dark sky, they saw it as a small star-like object. On occasion it appeared to be very bright, and it often showed a bit of color. By watching it night after night, people discovered that the object moved among the stars. They called it a wandering star.

They could also see other wanderers in the sky. Three of them moved rapidly. They were Mercury, Venus, and Mars. Two moved more slowly. These were Jupiter and Saturn, the farthest planets that can be seen without a telescope.

Today you can see Saturn just as people did thousands of years ago. You'll agree, it looks like a bright star.

Until 1610 people had seen Saturn only as a point of light, although by then they knew it was a planet and not a star. In that year Galileo, a famous Italian astronomer, looked at Saturn through a telescope. He was stunned. There were bulges on either side of the planet.

Galileo could not explain the bulges. He wrote that "Saturn has ears," for that's what the bulges looked like to him. Later, when Galileo looked at Saturn again, the bulges were gone. That must really have puzzled him, for this time he wrote, "Has Saturn, perhaps, devoured his own children?"

HUYGENS' TELESCOPE

Later in the seventeenth century, other astronomers made bigger and better telescopes. One of them was the Dutch astronomer Christian Huygens. In 1659, using one of the more powerful telescopes of his day, he, too, saw the bulges of Saturn. He could see they were not ears. Nor were they moons, as Galileo had suggested when he had called them children. The bulges were made by a ring around the planet. The ring was not attached, but was completely separate from Saturn. This was an exciting discovery, for no one had imagined that such a thing could exist. Nor could anyone explain how or why there should be such a ring.

Huygens also made other discoveries. Earlier, in 1655, he had sighted Titan, the largest of all the satellites of Saturn. And he explained why the appearance of the ring changed during the nearly 30 years it takes Saturn to go around the Sun.

In those days Saturn was of special interest to people. Many even supposed there was life of some kind on the planet. Perhaps Huygens did, too, for he said that if there *were* people on Saturn, they would live quite differently from Earth people. Winters, for example, would be 15 years long, and they would be severely cold. He wondered if people could endure that long a period of icy weather.

CAN YOU IMAGINE 15 YEARS OF WINTER?

In the middle of the 1670s Giovanni Domenico Cassini, a French-Italian astronomer, found that Saturn's ring was not a single ring, as Huygens had thought. There were, in fact, two rings. And they seemed to be separated by a gap, which ever since has been called the Cassini division. Later, other astronomers could see at least three rings.

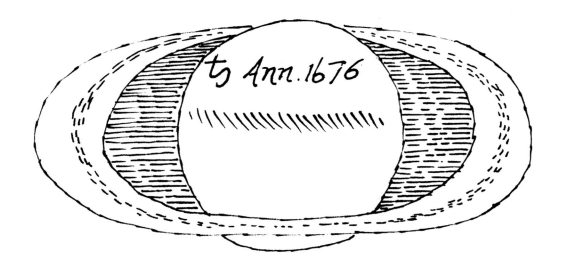

As telescopes improved through the centuries, more and more information about Saturn was gathered. For example, it was found that the planet has a diameter of about 120,000 kilometers, that it is made almost entirely of gases, and that the temperature of Saturn is very low—at least 175 degrees Celsius below zero.

Astronomers also discovered that Saturn had many more satellites than the one Huygens saw. Cassini found four. A hundred years later William Herschel, an English astronomer, found two more; in 1848 George Bond, an American sky mapper at Harvard, discovered one, and in 1898 William H. Pickering, another American, found another one. The tenth satellite discovered by using Earth-based telescopes was sighted by Audouin Dollfus, a French astronomer, in 1966. Later, when probes traveled close to Saturn, this satellite turned out to be two satellites. That's one thing we learned from the space probes. They also told us a lot more about this queen of the planets.

PIONEER AND VOYAGER

Pioneer and *Voyager* are the names of the unmanned spacecraft that explored Jupiter and Saturn in the late 1970s and early 1980s. On board the craft were cameras to take pictures of the planets and their satellites. There were instruments to measure the magnetism of the planets, to find out what gases surrounded them, and to measure their temperatures. There was also a plutonium electric generator to make electricity for the instruments, and for the radios that sent the information back to Earth.

In 1979, after a journey of several billion kilometers, *Pioneer* came within 21,400 kilometers of the tops of Saturn's clouds. *Voyagers 1* and *2*, which were launched in 1977, moved in even closer to Saturn in 1980 and 1981. These probes gave us more information about Saturn than had been gathered in the three hundred and seventy years since Galileo first saw the planet through a telescope.

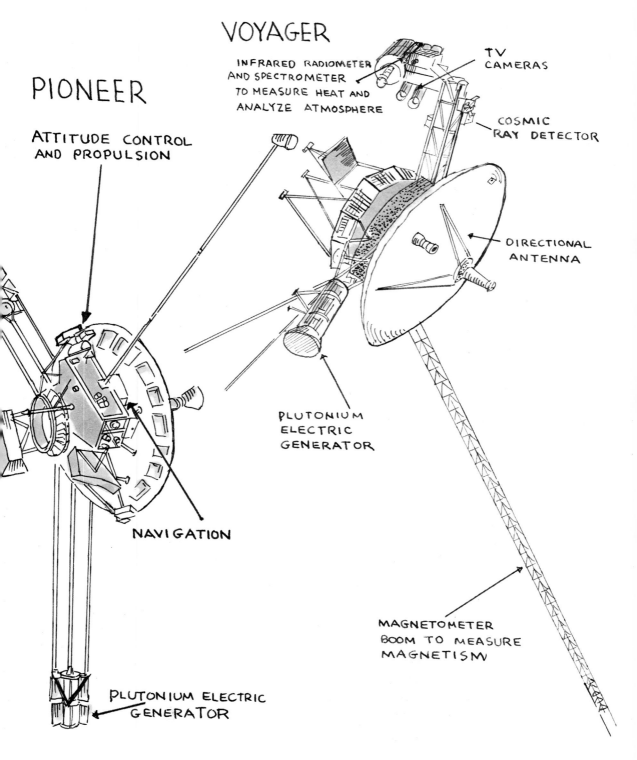

VOYAGER

PIONEER

INFRARED RADIOMETER
AND SPECTROMETER
TO MEASURE HEAT AND
ANALYZE ATMOSPHERE

TV
CAMERAS

ATTITUDE CONTROL
AND PROPULSION

COSMIC
RAY DETECTOR

DIRECTIONAL
ANTENNA

PLUTONIUM
ELECTRIC
GENERATOR

NAVIGATION

MAGNETOMETER
BOOM TO MEASURE
MAGNETISM

PLUTONIUM ELECTRIC
GENERATOR

9

THE SIZE AND SHAPE OF SATURN

Saturn is a huge planet. Of all the nine planets, only Jupiter is larger. The drawing shows how large Saturn would be if Earth were one centimeter across. If Saturn were hollow, more than 760 Earths could fit inside it.

Saturn is not round like a baseball. It is more the shape of a beach ball when you sit on it. Saturn is a flattened ball. So are most of the other planets—all except Mercury, Venus, and Pluto.

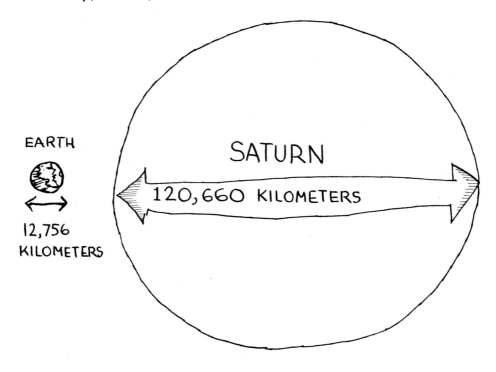

EARTH

12,756 KILOMETERS

SATURN

120,660 KILOMETERS

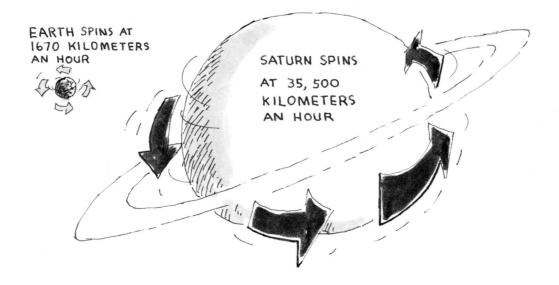

EARTH SPINS AT
1670 KILOMETERS
AN HOUR

SATURN SPINS
AT 35,500
KILOMETERS
AN HOUR

Earth is flattened, but not as much as Saturn. At the equator, the diameter of Earth is 12,756 kilometers. From the North Pole to the South Pole, the diameter is about 40 kilometers less. The bulge along the equator is caused by the spinning of the Earth.

Saturn spins much faster than we do. Earth spins at 1,670 kilometers an hour, while Saturn turns at a speed of 35,500 kilometers an hour. The speed with which it turns and the fact that it is composed largely of gases are what make Saturn the flattest of all the planets. At its equator Saturn has a diameter of 120,660 kilometers, 11,000 kilometers more than the diameter from pole to pole.

ROTATION AND REVOLUTION

Each of the nine planets spins on its axis. It takes Earth 24 hours to make a complete rotation. Saturn spins around once in just over 10½ hours. Only Jupiter takes less time to make one rotation.

Saturn rotates faster than most of the planets, but it moves very slowly as it travels around the Sun. It takes Earth a little over 365 days to go around the Sun once.

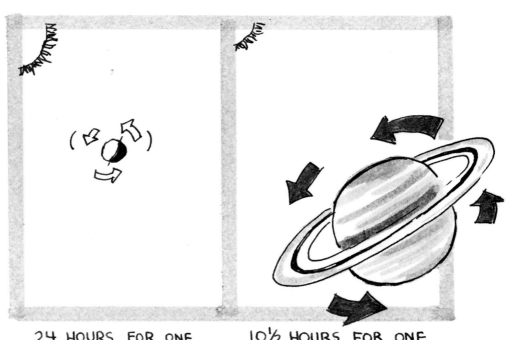

24 HOURS FOR ONE
ROTATION

10½ HOURS FOR ONE
ROTATION

EARTH ⚪   ☼ SUN

365 DAYS FOR EARTH TO TRAVEL AROUND THE SUN

29½ YEARS FOR SATURN TO TRAVEL AROUND THE SUN

It takes Saturn about 29½ years to make a complete revolution. That means that one year on Saturn would be almost 11,000 Earth days long.

Of all the planets known to people long ago, Saturn took the longest time to move across the sky. The Greeks named the planet Kronos, which means time. Of course, now we know of three other planets—Uranus, Neptune, and Pluto—that take even longer than Saturn to go around the Sun.

HEAT AND TEMPERATURE

The Sun provides heat for all the planets, so you would expect Mercury and Venus, the planets closest to the Sun, to be the hottest. And they are.

But while Mercury, the closest planet of all, gets very hot in the daytime, it loses heat very fast at night. Venus, though it is the second closest planet to the Sun, is hotter than Mercury. It stays very hot both day and night. That is because the atmosphere of Venus is made up mostly of carbon dioxide, a gas that traps heat and keeps it from escaping.

At our distance from the sun—about 150 million kilo-

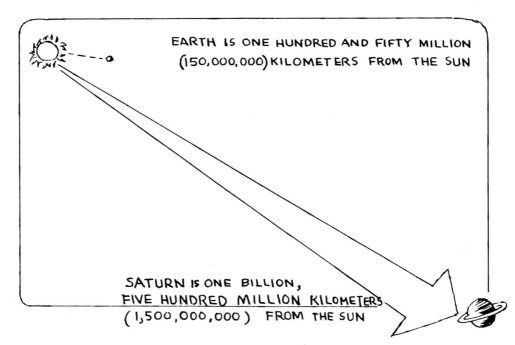

EARTH IS ONE HUNDRED AND FIFTY MILLION (150,000,000) KILOMETERS FROM THE SUN

SATURN IS ONE BILLION, FIVE HUNDRED MILLION KILOMETERS (1,500,000,000) FROM THE SUN

meters—we don't get too hot in the daytime or too cold at night. The average temperature on Earth is about 14 degrees Celsius.

Saturn, though, is almost one billion five hundred million kilometers from the Sun, ten times farther away than Earth. It is so far away that it receives much less heat from the Sun than we do. In the gases that surround Saturn, temperatures hover around 175 degrees Celsius below zero. That's unbelievably cold. The coldest place on Earth is only 88 degrees Celsius below zero.

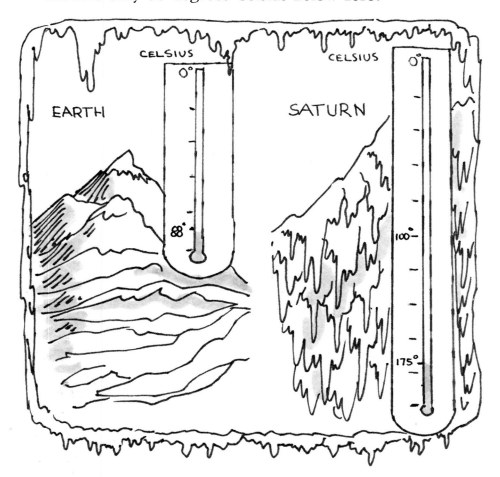

But because of its distance from the Sun, Saturn should be even colder than it is. The planet is giving off more heat than it receives. This is one of the puzzles about Saturn that scientists are trying to solve. Where does the extra heat come from?

Some people think they know at least part of the answer. The extra heat, they say, was generated billions of years ago when the planet formed. The gases and other materials from which Saturn is made came together with great force. The force was large enough to produce tremendous amounts of heat, heat that is still trapped beneath the heavy clouds of gases that surround the planet. Slowly, some of the heat works through to the surface and then escapes into space. Earth was probably formed in the same way as Saturn, and heat was generated here also. But our planet has lost most of its heat of formation. The heat has been able to escape through our atmosphere.

Another possible explanation is that the extra heat of Saturn is generated by friction, caused by liquid helium sinking through liquid hydrogen. This occurs deep in the interior of the planet. The *Voyager* probes showed us that there is less helium in Saturn's atmosphere than we expected—a fact that supports this second theory.

DENSITY, MASS, AND GRAVITY

Astronomers describe the planets in many different ways—by size, for example, by temperature, and by distance from the Sun. They also describe the planets by density.

Density tells us how tightly the materials in something are packed together. In a solid material, such as rock or metal, the molecules are packed together closely, more closely than in water or in other liquids. In turn, the molecules in a liquid are packed together more tightly than they are in gases, such as oxygen or carbon dioxide.

The density of something is usually measured by comparing it to water. Water is given a density of 1. If the molecules and atoms in a substance are packed together more tightly than those in water, its density would be more than 1. Should the materials be packed together less tightly, the density would be less than 1.

The density of Earth is 5.52—the highest density of all the planets. The density of Saturn is 0.69, less than the density of water. Because of its low density, Saturn would float on water—if there were an ocean large enough to hold the planet.

	EARTH	SATURN
Density	5.52	.69
Mass	1	95.2

Another way of measuring a planet, or comparing it to the other planets, is by its mass. That's an indication of the amount of material it contains. Usually the mass of a planet is measured by comparing it to the mass of Earth, which is given a value of 1. Mercury, Venus, Mars, and Pluto have masses less than 1. They contain less material than Earth does. Pluto has a mass of 0.0019, the lowest of all the planets. Saturn has a mass of 95.2, meaning that it contains 95.2 times more material than Earth does.

Yet another way to describe a planet is by its gravitation. Gravity is the force that holds you in a chair, makes a ball you throw fall to the ground, and brings the space shuttle back to Earth. It pulls everything down toward the center of the Earth. In the same way, the gravity of Saturn pulls everything toward the center of Saturn.

GRAVITATIONAL FORCE

ON EARTH   ON SATURN

Gravity is a force that depends upon mass and upon the distance from the surface to the center of a planet. Where there is less mass, a planet's gravity would be less than ours. The gravity on Mercury and Mars is less than half that on Earth. Jupiter, Saturn, Uranus, and Neptune have gravities that are somewhat greater than the gravity on Earth. The gravity of Saturn is 1.13 times what it is here.

Your weight is a measure of the amount of gravity pulling you down. On Mercury and Mars you would weigh less than half as much as you do on Earth. On Saturn you would weigh slightly more. If you weigh 100 pounds at Earth's equator, you would weigh 113 pounds at Saturn's.

THE LAYERS OF SATURN

Earth is called a solid planet. It is made mostly of rocks and metals. Saturn, on the other hand, is made mostly of gases and liquids. It is called a gaseous planet.

The Earth's atmosphere is about 50 kilometers deep, though traces of it are found as far out as 1,000 kilometers. Our atmosphere is a mixture of many gases, but mostly it is made of nitrogen and oxygen. Beneath the atmosphere is the solid part of Earth.

Saturn has a much deeper atmosphere. It is probably 30,000 kilometers deep. The gases are mostly hydrogen and helium.

EARTH'S
ATMOSPHERE
IS ALMOST
50 KILOMETERS
DEEP

SATURN'S ATMOSPHERE IS ALMOST
30,000 KILOMETERS DEEP

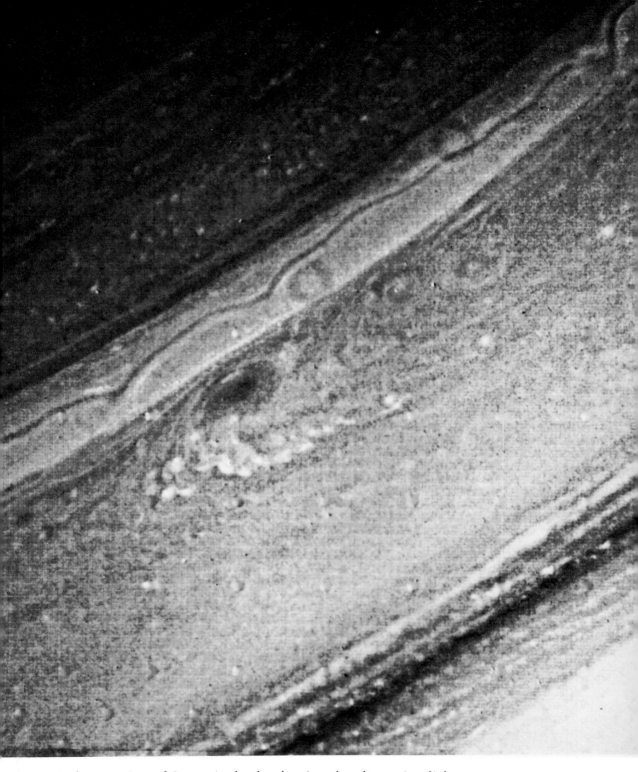

*A close-up view of Saturn's clouds, showing the alternating light
and dark belts or bands of gases.*

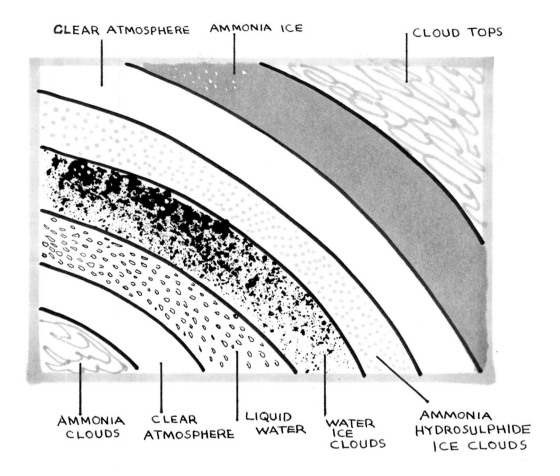

CLEAR ATMOSPHERE   AMMONIA ICE   CLOUD TOPS

AMMONIA CLOUDS   CLEAR ATMOSPHERE   LIQUID WATER   WATER ICE CLOUDS   AMMONIA HYDROSULPHIDE ICE CLOUDS

Through the upper part of Saturn's atmosphere, we can see alternating light and dark belts, many of which appear to go all around the planet. You can see them in practically every photograph of Saturn. These are thin layers of clouds made up of various amounts of ammonia, water, and methane. Because it is so cold on Saturn, the materials in the clouds are mostly frozen.

23

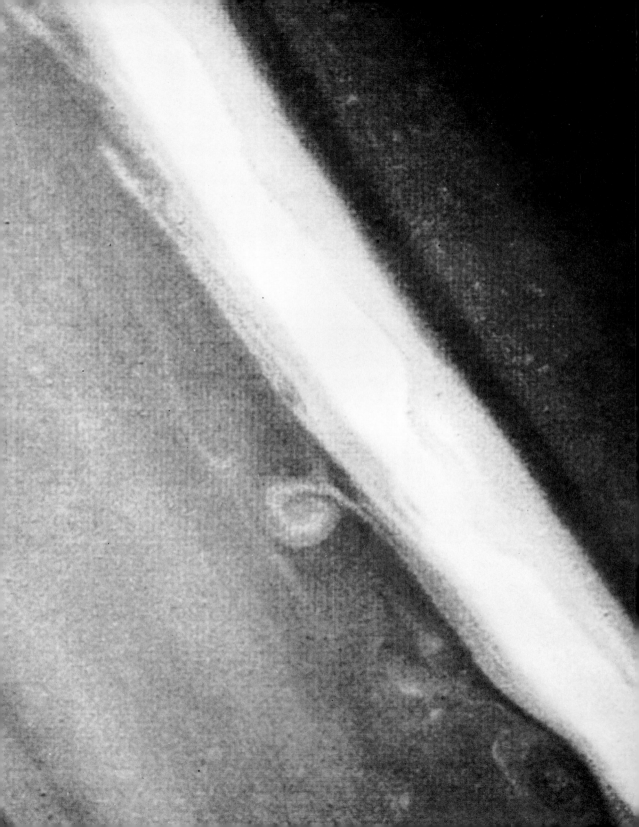

The *Voyager* probes found that along Saturn's equator the clouds, and very likely the surrounding atmosphere as well, blow at speeds up to 480 meters a second—that's 1,100 miles an hour. The fastest winds on Earth blow about 300 miles an hour. And it seems that the winds on Saturn blow constantly.

You and I could not survive in the atmosphere of Saturn. Nor could any other living thing, either plant or animal.

Beneath Saturn's atmosphere there are probably regions where the hydrogen and helium become liquids. The layers above push down on the gases, causing them to change to liquids. (If the pressure here on Earth were much higher, the air surrounding us would turn into a liquid—there would be liquid air.)

Deep inside Saturn the pressure is thousands of times greater than it is on Earth. The liquid hydrogen is compressed so much that, even though it is still liquid, it behaves like a metal. For example, it can conduct electricity. It is called liquid metallic hydrogen. Farther in, at

Another close-up view of the clouds. Notice the swirl at the center of the photograph. This was produced by the movement of the clouds.

the very center of Saturn, there may be a core of solid material. If there is, it would probably be no larger than twice the size of Earth, and perhaps it would be much smaller.

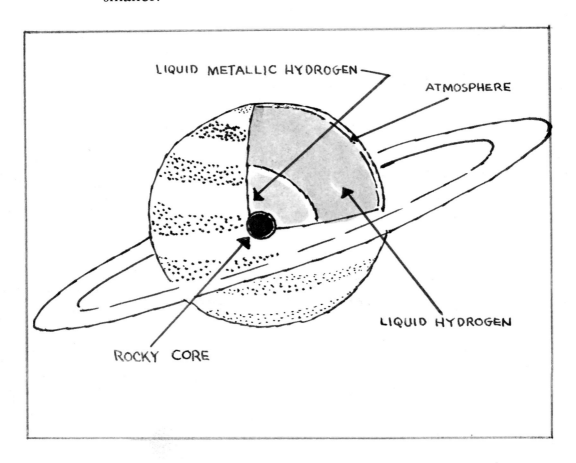

A color-enhanced photograph of Saturn (right), taken when Voyager 2 was 43 million kilometers from the planet.

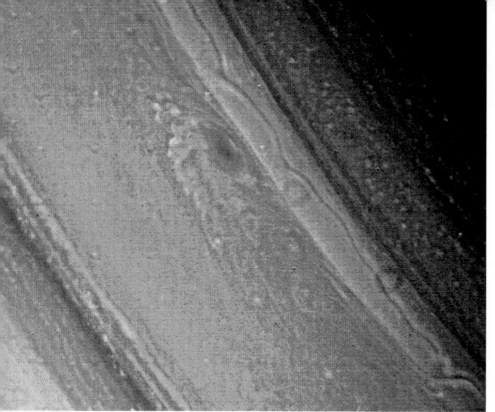

*Saturn's
atmosphere,
close-up*

Saturn's rings

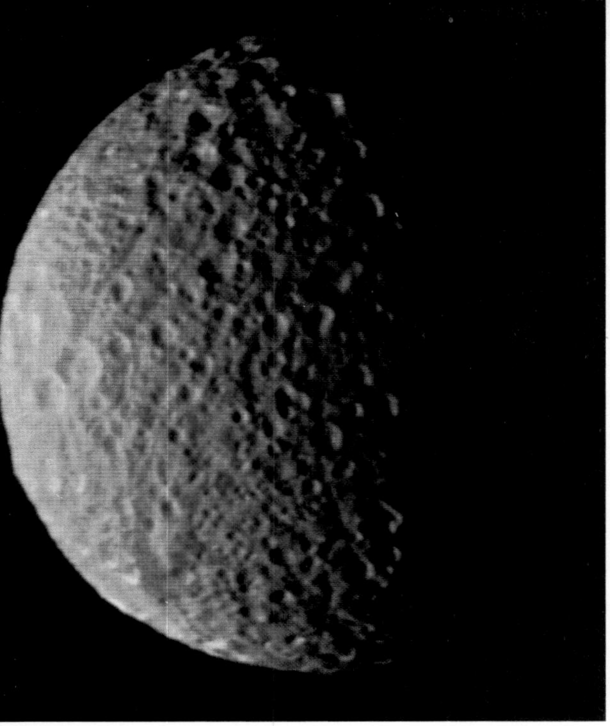

Mimas

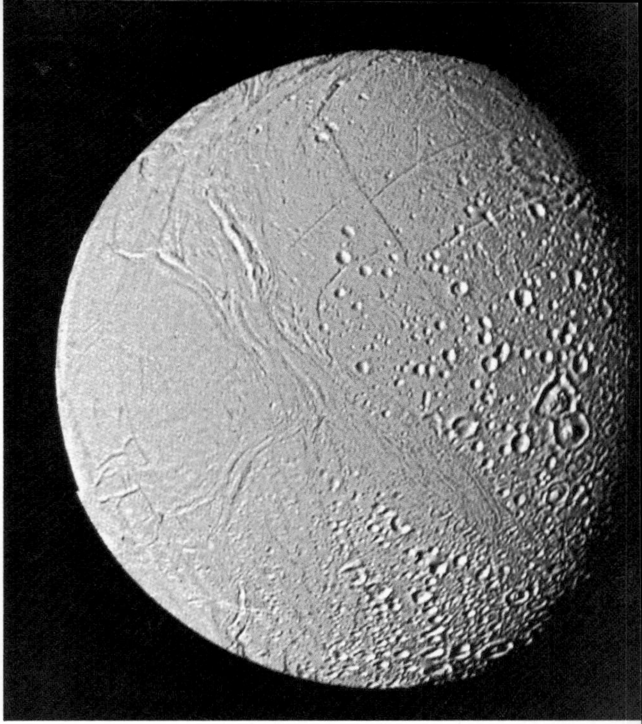

Enceladus

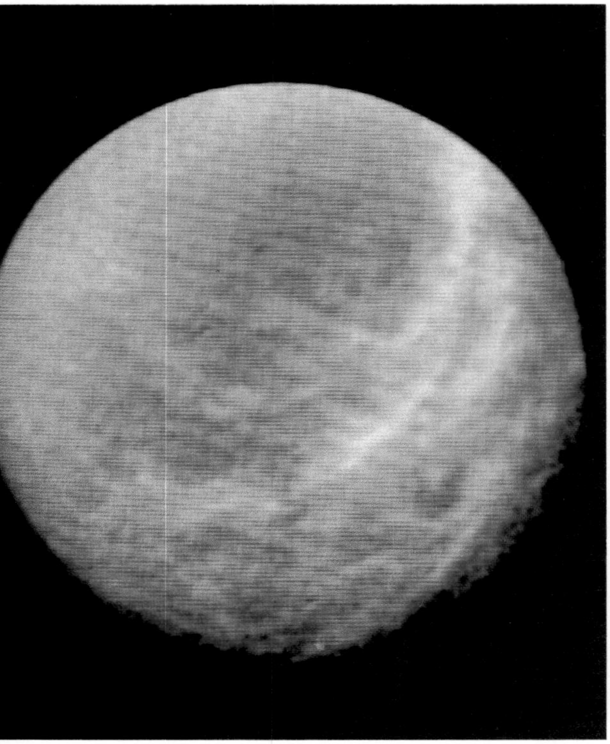

Rhea

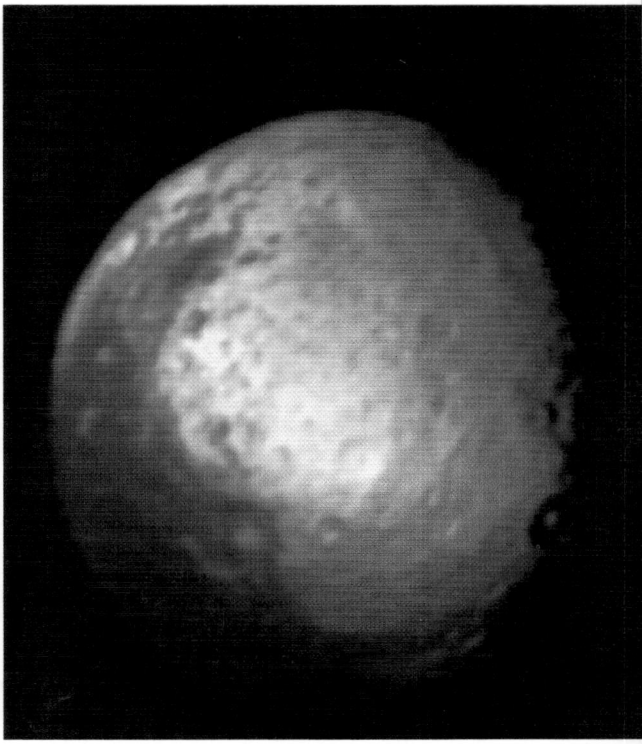

Iapetus

Voyager 2 *began its 2.25 billion kilometer journey on the launching pad at Cape Kennedy in Florida.*

An artist's view of Saturn and some of its satellites, prepared from individual photographs. Dione is in the foreground. Tethys and Mimas are in the distance at the lower right. Enceladus and Rhea are at the left, and Titan is at the top right.

THE RINGS OF SATURN

Before *Pioneer* and *Voyager,* when our best view was through an Earth-based telescope, we thought Saturn had three rings, or perhaps four. Some scientists thought they could see six of them. But now we know there are many more rings, perhaps thousands of them. And they are more complex than anyone suspected.

Rings thought to be single formations turned out to be made of many smaller rings. And many dim rings were found, ones that Earth-based astronomers could never have hoped to see even with the most powerful telescopes. Someone has said the rings are so close together, and there are so many of them, they look very much like the grooves in a phonograph record.

Many of the rings are made of very small particles. For the most part they appear to be pieces of ice mixed with bits of solid ash and dust. Some of the rings may contain larger particles—chunks of ice and possibly rock and metal—that are several meters or more across.

The ring system is huge. The diameter of the entire system, from outer edge to outer edge, may be as much

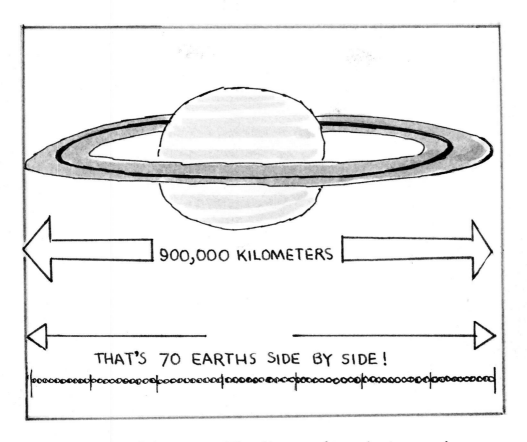

as 900,000 kilometers. The distance from the inner edge of the innermost ring to the outer edge of the outermost is at least 240,000 kilometers.

The rings are not very thick. At the thickest part most of them probably do not exceed 5 kilometers, and some are much thinner than 150 meters. However, one of them may be 1,000 kilometers or more in thickness.

A close-up view of the rings.

THEORIES ABOUT THE RINGS

No one knows how and when the rings of Saturn formed. This remains one of the great mysteries about the planet. And recently the mystery became even deeper when rings were discovered around both Jupiter and Uranus.

Saturn, like the rest of the planets, is perhaps four and a half billion years old. And the rings are probably the same age. It is believed that around that time, great clouds of gases, dust, and ash packed together. The largest masses became planets. It's possible that some material was not packed into the planet itself. And this "leftover" material may now compose the satellites of the planet and the rings.

Perhaps particles in the rings are occasionally pulled into the planet. If so, the rings would gradually lose material to the planet. Eventually Saturn may have no rings. The planet may still be in the process of forming.

Saturn and two of its satellites, Tethys (above) and Dione (below). Notice the shadows cast by the rings. Notice also the gaps between the rings. You can see the surface of the planet through the gaps.

Perhaps this has happened to other planets as well, including our own. It may be that all planets have rings during some stage in their development. And after millions of years they lose them. That's one theory used to explain the rings of Saturn, and of Jupiter and Uranus.

Another theory suggests that the rings of planets form when a satellite moves closer to the planet. Because of slight variations in gravitation, the distances between a satellite and its planet do change. Over millions of years the two may move considerably farther apart or closer together.

A satellite of Saturn may have moved closer to the planet. If it did, Saturn's gravitational pull would have been strong enough to raise a bulge on the satellite. Earth's gravity, for example, has produced a bulge on the Moon. In the case of Saturn's satellite, the bulge may have become larger and larger. Finally it became so large that the entire satellite shattered, breaking up into ice and dust. Eventually the separate particles formed into rings.

No one knows whether either of the two theories is correct. There may well be an entirely different explanation for the rings. It's only one of many questions that scientists have about Saturn.

SATURN'S SATELLITES

Space probes have revealed that Saturn has many more satellites than we thought. Observers at telescopes on Earth found four while the *Voyager* probes were on their way to Saturn, and photographs made by the probes revealed eight more. Now we believe there are twenty-two. And there may be others.

On page 36 is a list of the satellites that have been discovered so far, some information about them, the person or probe that found them, and the year they were sighted. The names of some of the satellites are taken from gods of the harvest, whom the Romans connected with Saturn, their god of reaping.

Except for Titan and Phoebe, all of Saturn's satellites are covered with water ice. In some cases they seem to be made almost entirely of ice.

Most are round, but some of those most recently discovered, the very small ones, are not. They look something like potatoes. They may be halves of satellites that broke in two, or they may be the remains of larger satellites that broke apart into many pieces.

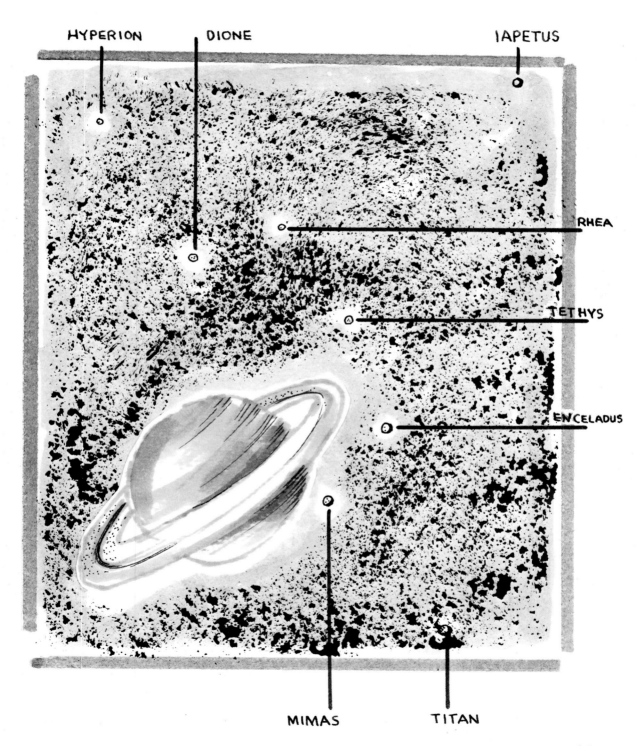

HYPERION

DIONE

IAPETUS

RHEA

TETHYS

ENCELADUS

MIMAS

TITAN

35

NAME	DIAMETER (km)	DISTANCE FROM PLANET (1000s of km)	PERIOD OF REVOLUTION (days hrs)	DISCOVERER AND DATE
1980S28	40×20	138	14.4h	*Voyager 1*, 1980
1980S27	140×100	139	14.7h	*Voyager 1*, 1980
1980S26	110×90	142	15.1h	*Voyager 1*, 1980
1980S1	220×200	151	16.7h	Audoin Dollfus, 1966
1980S3	140×120	151	16.7h	J.W. Fountain and S. M. Larson, 1977
Mimas	392	186	22.6h	William Herschel, 1789
1981S12	10	186	22.6h	*Voyager 2*, 1981
Enceladus	500	238	1d 8.9h	William Herschel, 1789
Tethys	1060	295	1d 21.3h	Giovanni Cassini, 1684
1980S13	34×28	295	1d 21.3h	Smith & Larson & Reitsema, 1980
1980S25	34×22	295	1d 21.3h	Space Telescope Camera, 1980
1981S6	20	295	1d 21.3h	*Voyager 2*, 1981
1981S11	15	350	2d 10.6h	*Voyager 2*, 1981
Dione	1120	377	2d 17.7h	Giovanni Cassini, 1684
1980S6	36×32	377	2d 17.7h	P. Laques and J. Lecacheux, 1980
1981S7	20	377	2d 17.7h	*Voyager 2*, 1981
1981S9	15	470	3d 19h	*Voyager 2*, 1981
Rhea	1,530	527	4d 12.4h	Giovanni Cassini, 1672
Titan	5,800 (atmos.) 5,150 (surf.)	1,222	15d 22.7h	Christian Huygens, 1655
Hyperion	410×260	1,481	21d 6.6h	George Bond, 1848
Iapetus	1,460	3,561	79d 7.9h	Giovanni Cassini, 1671
Phoebe	220	12,954	550d 10.8h	William H. Pickering, 1898

Until they are officially named, satellites are numbered with the year and order of sighting.
Approximate equatorial and pole-to-pole diameters are given.

Almost all of the satellites have many craters on their surfaces. The craters vary in size and number from one satellite to another. Mimas has a huge crater. It is one fourth the diameter of the entire satellite. Whatever hit the satellite—it might have been another satellite, or an asteroid or a comet—must have done so with so much force it nearly broke Mimas apart. There is also a huge crater on Tethys, though it is not as deep as the one on Mimas.

The huge crater on Mimas has raised edges and a central peak. If the impact of whatever hit it had been just a bit greater, Mimas probably would have been broken in two by the collision.

ENCELADUS, shown earlier in this book in a color photograph, shines most brightly of all Saturn's satellites. That's because its rather smooth surface reflects more light than any of the other satellites. Perhaps volcanoes have erupted on Enceladus and the flowing lava smoothed its hills and valleys. There are ridges and small craters on the surface, but no large craters. Or it may be that Saturn and the satellite Dione exert a strong gravitational pull on Enceladus, causing its surface ice to heave and melt together. The tides would raise and then lower the surface ice. This would cause heating in much the way a piece of wire gets hot when you bend it back and forth.

TETHYS has very deep, bowl-shaped craters on its surface, much like those on Mimas. Like the other satellites, it seems to be made almost entirely of water ice. There is a valley on Tethys' surface that is over two thousand kilometers long and a hundred kilometers wide. It may have been made billions of years ago as the icy satellite froze solid.

Two views of Tethys, one (top) showing the jagged valley that may extend for more than 2000 kilometers, the other (bottom) showing Tethys' many craters.

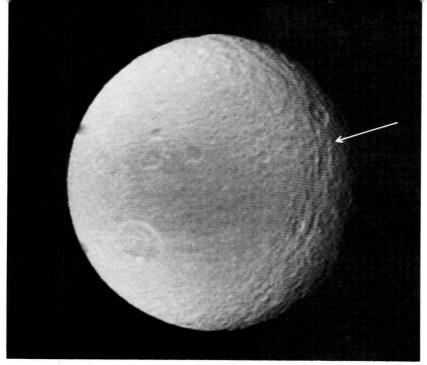

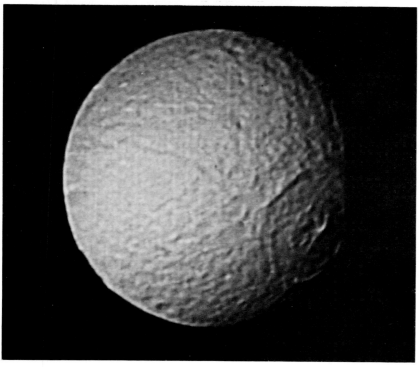

DIONE has a diameter only slightly larger than that of Tethys. But its density is greater, causing scientists to believe the satellite has more rock in it than Tethys. Dione's surface shows large, whitish regions. These seem to be breaks in the crust where water has escaped from the interior and frozen into frost. Also, the surface seems to have gone through changes. Mostly it is covered with craters, but here and there it is smoothed out. As yet, no one knows how this might have happened.

Two views of Dione, showing its whitish regions and (right) a heavily cratered section of its surface.

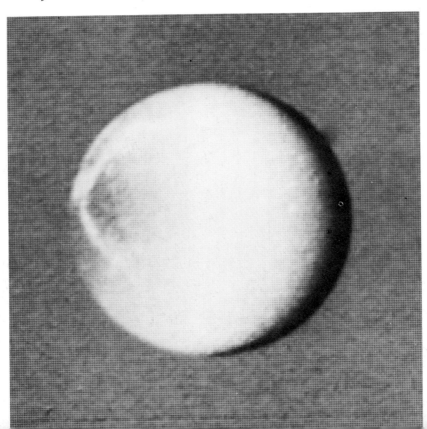

RHEA, shown earlier in color, is also made of rock and ice. It is about two and a half times larger than Dione. Its surface is also rougher. There are craters and grooves. Like Dione's, large areas seem to be frost covered. The temperature, as on the other satellites, is incredibly low. In sunshine it is about 175 degrees Celsius below zero. As Rhea moved into Saturn's shadow, *Voyager* instruments recorded a temperature of minus 220 degrees Celsius.

TITAN, with a diameter of 5,150 kilometers, is the largest of Saturn's satellites. In fact, if we include its layer of atmosphere, Titan has a diameter of 5,800 kilometers, making it the largest satellite in the entire solar system. Titan is even larger than the planets Mercury and Pluto. Also, it is the only satellite in the solar system known to have a considerable atmosphere.

Because Titan is covered with haze, its surface cannot be seen. Its density is twice that of water, so Titan is probably half rock and half water.

It's cold on Titan, at least 175 degrees below zero. Most of the satellite's atmosphere—probably 90 percent—is nitrogen, and the rest is mostly methane and argon. There is a trace of hydrogen cyanide. All in all, its air would be most unpleasant to breathe. In fact it

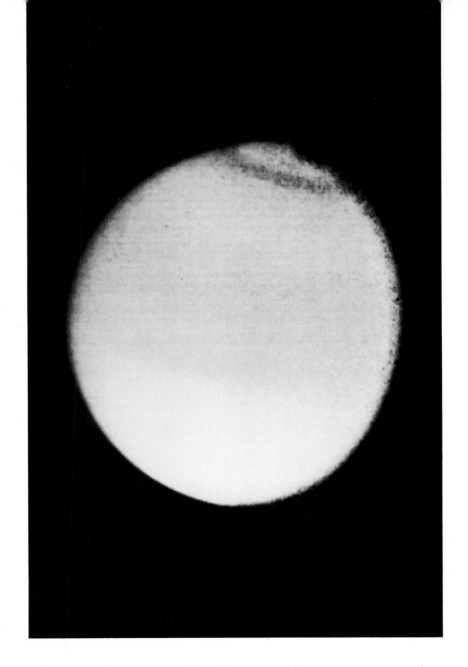

The atmosphere surrounding Titan is so dense we cannot see the surface of the satellite. Notice that some parts of the atmosphere appear darker than others.

would be poisonous to any creature we can imagine.

Because of its dense atmosphere, people used to think it possible that at some time life would appear on Titan. However, now that we know the atmosphere contains poisonous gases, and that the satellite is a super-refrigerator, those ideas are not very popular. Also, oxygen has not been detected. Earth remains the only place in the universe where we are certain there are living plants and animals.

HYPERION was believed to have a diameter of 290 kilometers. But it turned out to be larger in one direction and smaller in the other. It is shaped somewhat like a dented dill pickle. It measures 410 kilometers the long way and 220 to 260 kilometers in the shorter dimension. It is likely that at one time Hyperion was larger. It has been bombarded by pieces of rock and metal that have been in orbit around Saturn for millions of years. Some of these collisions may well have been strong enough to break apart the once larger satellite. Hyperion is all that is left.

Three views of Hyperion taken at different times as Voyager 2 *flew by the satellite. Hyperion is irregular in shape and has a heavily cratered surface.*

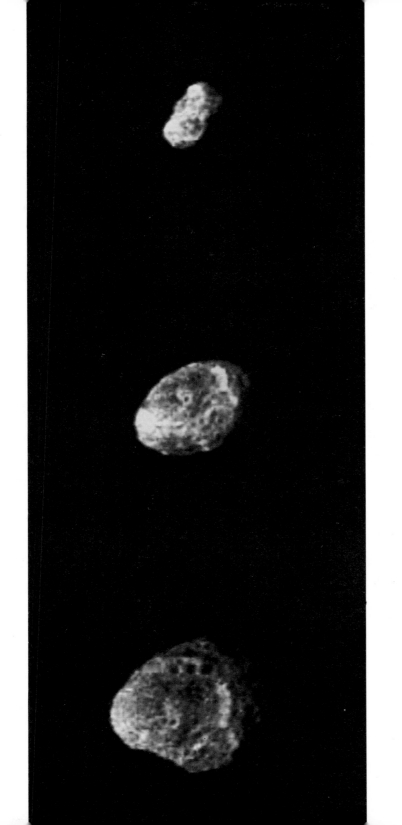

IAPETUS is especially strange in that one half of it appears to be much brighter than the other half. As you can see in the color photograph earlier in this book, the boundary between the two parts is curved. It is not an even line. Very likely the surface of the bright area is ice. The darker area is somewhat reddish. Perhaps here the ice has worn away and darker rocks have been exposed. Possibly the darker area is covered with debris that surged to the surface during volcanic eruptions.

PHOEBE is the most remote of Saturn's satellites. It is almost 13 million kilometers from the planet. This tiny object takes 550 days to circle Saturn. Alone among Saturn's satellites, it revolves backward, moving westward among the stars rather than eastward. It also has the darkest surface of all Saturn's satellites.

Instead of keeping its same face toward Saturn like the other satellites, it spins once every 9 hours. Such facts lead scientists to believe that Phoebe was not originally a satellite of Saturn. Rather, they believe it was an asteroid that was caught by Saturn's gravity when at some time in the past it passed too close to the planet.

PHOEBE

13 MILLION KILOMETERS

FINDING SATURN IN THE
NIGHT SKY

Saturn is a fairly easy planet to find. Under "Planets" in an almanac you'll find the months and days when the planet can be seen, in the evening or early in the morning. Or look up a section called "Celestial Events" in *Natural History* magazine. There you will see directions for finding the planets. There is also a sky map to help you.

When a planet is especially bright and easy to find, radio stations also may give directions for locating it. So keep listening and looking.

Without a telescope you won't be able to see any of Saturn's rings or satellites, or any details of the surface of

Looking back—a photograph taken four days after
Voyager 1 *flew past Saturn. Night shadows*
fall across the planet and its rings. On the right,
one can see the shadows that the denser rings
cast on the planet.

the planet. But you will see Saturn as a fairly bright
object. Someday you may get a chance to look at Saturn
through a high-power telescope. Then you'll be able to
see the rings. When you do, we think you'll agree that
Saturn is truly a rare beauty. Small wonder it is called
Queen of the Planets.

Facts about Saturn

	SATURN	EARTH
Distance from Sun (Millions of kilometers)		
Mean	1427	149.6
Greatest	1506	152.1
Least	1348	147.1
Period of revolution	29.46 years	365.26 days
Speed in orbit (revolution) (Km per second)	9.65	29.8
Period of rotation	$10^h39^m24^s$	$23^h56^m04^s$
Speed of rotation (Km per hour)	35,500	1,670
Inclination of axis	26°44'	23°27'
Atmosphere main elements	hydrogen, helium	nitrogen, oxygen
Mean temperature °C	−175	14
Volume (Earth = 1)	769	1
Satellites	22 (probably more)	1
Equatorial diameter (Kilometers)	120,660	12,756
Mass (Earth = 1)	95.2	1
Density (Water = 1)	0.69	5.52
Surface gravity (Earth = 1)	1.13	1

INDEX

(Page numbers in italic refer to photographs)

almanacs, planets' appearances
listed in, 48
ammonia, in Saturn's cloud
belts, 23
argon, in Titan's atmosphere, 42
asteroids
collisions between planets
and, 37
in Saturn's orbit, 46

carbon dioxide
properties of, 14, 17
in Venus's atmosphere, 14
Cassini, Giovanni Domenico, 6
satellites discovered by, 7,
36
Cassini division, 6
cloud belts of Saturn, 22–25,
22, 24
composition of, 23
heat trapped by, 16
winds in, 25
comets, 37
craters, causes of, 37, 38

density, 17–20
of Dione, 40
of Earth, 17

of gases, 17
of liquids, 17
of Saturn, 17
of solids, 17
of Tethys, 40
of Titan, 42
of water, 17
Dione, *31,* 40–41, *40–41*
density of, 40
diameter of, 36, 40
discovery of, 36
distance from Saturn of, 36
Enceladus's surface ice and,
38
period of, 36
size of, 42
surface of, 40–41, 42
see also satellites of Saturn
Dollfus, Audouin, 7, 36

Earth
atmosphere of, 21
density of, 17
depth of atmosphere of, 21
distance from Sun of, 14
flattened shape of, 11
formation of, 16
gravity on, 19

Earth *(cont.)*
    mass of, 18
    Moon's bulge and, 32
    pressure in atmosphere of,
      25
    revolution of, 12–13
    rotation of, 11
    size of, 10
    spinning of, 11
    temperature of, 15
    wind speed on, 25
Enceladus, 38, *color insert*
    in orbit, 35
    surface of, 38
    see also satellites of Saturn

Galileo Galilei, 3, 4
gaseous planets, 21
gases, density of, 17
gods, Roman, 34
gravity, 19–20
    on Earth, 19
    on Mars, 20
    mass and, 20
    on Mercury, 20
    weight and, 20
Greeks, ancient, 13

helium
    hydrogen and, 16
    as liquid, 25
    in Saturn's atmosphere, 16,
      21, 25

Herschel, William, 7, 36
Huygens, Christian, 4–5, 6, 7
    discoveries of, 4, 36
hydrogen
    as liquid, 25
    in Saturn's atmosphere, 16,
      21, 25
    sinking of helium through,
      16
hydrogen cyanide, in Titan's
    atmosphere, 42
Hyperion, 44–45, *44*
    diameter of, 36
    discovery of, 36
    distance from Saturn of, 36
    in orbit, 35
    period of, 36
    shape of, 44–45, *44*
    surface of, 44–45, *44*
    see also satellites of Saturn

Iapetus, 46, *color insert*
    diameter of, 36
    discovery of, 36
    distance from Saturn of, 36
    in orbit, 35
    period of, 36
    variations in brightness of, 46
    see also satellites of Saturn

Jupiter
    rings of, 30–32
    rotation of, 12

Jupiter *(cont.)*
  size of, 10
  space probes of, 8
  storms on, 1
  as wandering star, 2

Kronos, 13

life, extraterrestrial
  on Saturn, 5
  on Titan, 44
liquid metallic hydrogen, 25
liquids, density of, 17

Mars
  ancients' view of, 2
  gravity on, 20
  mass of, 18
  surface of, 1
mass, 18
  of Earth, 18
  gravity and, 20
  of Mars, 18
  of Mercury, 18
  of Pluto, 18
  of Saturn, 18
  of Venus, 18
Mercury
  ancients' view of, 2
  distance from Sun of, 14
  gravity on, 20
  mass of, 18
  shape of, 10

surface of, 1
  temperature of, 14
  Titan's size vs. size of, 42
methane
  in Saturn's cloud belt, 23
  in Titan's atmosphere, 42
Mimas, 37, *37, color insert*
  crater on, 37, *37*
  diameter of, 36
  discovery of, 36
  distance from Saturn of, 36
  in orbit, 35
  period of, 36
  see also satellites of Saturn
Moon, Earth's gravity and, 32
moons of Saturn, *see* satellites
  of Saturn

Natural History, 48
Neptune, revolution of, 13
nitrogen
  in Earth's atmosphere, 21
  in Titan's atmosphere, 42

oxygen
  density of, 17
  in Earth's atmosphere, 21

Phoebe, 34, 46–47
  diameter of, 36
  discovery of, 36
  distance from Saturn of, 36,
    46–47

Phoebe *(cont.)*
   period of, 36
   revolution of, 46–47
   surface of, 46
   see also satellites of Saturn
Pickering, William H., 7, 36
Pioneer space probe
   diagram of, 9
   instruments on, 8–9
   journey of, 8
   see also space probes
planets
   distances between satellites
      and, 32
   gaseous, 21
   largest of, 10
   lowest density of, 18
   rings of, 30–32
   sighting of, 48
   solid, 21
   see also specific planets
Pluto
   mass of, 18
   revolution of, 13
   shape of, 10
   Titan's size vs. size of, 42
plutonium-electric generators,
   8–9
   diagram of, 9

revolutions, 12–13
   of Neptune, 13
   of Phoebe, 46–47

of Pluto, 13
of Saturn, 12–13
of Saturn's satellites, 46
of Uranus, 13
Rhea, 42, *color insert*
   diameter of, 36
   discovery of, 36
   distance from Saturn of, 36
   in orbit, 35
   period of, 36
   size of, 42
   surface of, 42
   temperature of, 42
   see also satellites of Saturn
rings of Jupiter, 30–32
rings of Saturn, 27–33, *28,*
   color insert
   age of, 30
   close-up view of, 28
   composition of, 27
   diameter of system of,
      27–29
   discovery of, 3
   as "ears," 3
   formation of, 30–33
   gaps discovered in, 6
   loss of, 30–32
   number of, 1, 27
   shadows cast by, 30–31, *31,*
      48–49
   thickness of, 29
rings of Uranus, 30–32
Roman gods, 34

rotations, 12
  of Earth, 12
  of Jupiter, 12
  of Saturn, 12

satellites, distances between
    planets and, 32
satellites of Saturn, 34–47
  composition of, 30, 34
  craters on, 37
  darkest of, 46
  directions of revolutions of,
    46
  discoveries of, 4, 7, 36
  formation of, 30–33
  largest of, 42
  most remote of, 46
  number of, 7, 34
  shapes of, 34
  shattering of, 32–33, 34
  table of, 36
Saturn, *vi, 48, color insert*
  age of, 30
  ancients' view of, 2
  atmosphere of, 21–26, *color
    insert*
  composition of, 6, 11,
    25–26
  composition of atmosphere
    of, 21
  core of, 26
  density of, 17
  diameter of, 6, 11

distance from Sun of, 14, 15
"ears" of, 3
extra heat of, 16
flatness of, 10, 11
formation of, 16, 30–32
gravity on, 19–20
life on, 5
mass of, 18
pressure in atmosphere of,
    25–26
as Queen of the Planets, 50
revolution of, 12–13
rotation of, 11
sighting of, 48–50
size of, 10
spinning of, 11
temperature of, 6, 14–16,
    23
wind speed on, 25
winters on, 5
see also cloud belts of Saturn;
    rings of Saturn;
    satellites of Saturn
Saturn (Roman god), 34
sky maps, 48
solid planets, 21
solids, density of, 17
space probes, 1–2, 7, 8–9
  diagram of, 9
  Saturn's satellites discovered
    by, 34
  see also Pioneer space probe;
    Voyager space probes

space shuttle, gravity and, 19
Sun, heat provided by,
    14–15

telescopes, 3–6, 27, 34, 48
    early, 3–7
    improvement of, 7
    sighting planets without use
        of, 2–3, 48–50
Tethys, 31, 38–39, 39
    composition of, 38
    crater on, 37, 38–39
    density of, 40
    diameter of, 36, 40
    discovery of, 36
    distance from Saturn of, 36
    in orbit, 35
    period of, 36
    surface of, 38–39
    see also satellites of Saturn
Titan, 34, 42–44
    atmosphere of, 42–44, 43
    density of, 42
    diameter of, 36, 42
    discovery of, 4, 36
    distance from Saturn of, 36
    life on, 44
    in orbit, 35
    period of, 36
    see also satellites of Saturn

Uranus
    revolution of, 13
    rings of, 30–32

Venus
    ancients' view of, 2
    atmosphere of, 14
    clouds of, 1
    mass of, 18
    shape of, 10
    temperature of, 14
volcanic eruptions, 38, 46
Voyager space probes, 45,
        color insert
    diagram of, 9
    instruments on, 8–9
    journey of, 8
    Rhea's temperatures
        recorded by, 42
    Saturn's clouds and, 25
    Saturn's helium and, 16
    Saturn's satellites discovered
        by, 34, 36
    see also space probes

wandering stars, planets as, 2
water
    density of, 17
    in Saturn's cloud belts, 23
weight, gravity and, 20

Franklyn M. Branley is a man of many interests and accomplishments. Astronomer Emeritus and Former Chairman of the American Museum-Hayden Planetarium, he has written over 100 books on astronomy and other subjects for people of all ages. He is also coeditor of the Let's-Read-and-Find-Out Science book series.

Dr. Branley holds degrees from New York University, Columbia University, and the State University of New York College at New Paltz. He and his wife live in Sag Harbor, New York.

Leonard Kessler is the popular author and illustrator of scores of books for children, and a designer and painter as well. He first became interested in children's books as a result of teaching art to young people.

Mr. Kessler was graduated from Carnegie-Mellon University with a degree in fine arts, painting, and design. He lives in New York City, New York.

J 523.46 B   45611
BRANLEY, FRANKLYN
SATURN : THE SPECTACULAR
PLANET

DISCARD